SPIDERS

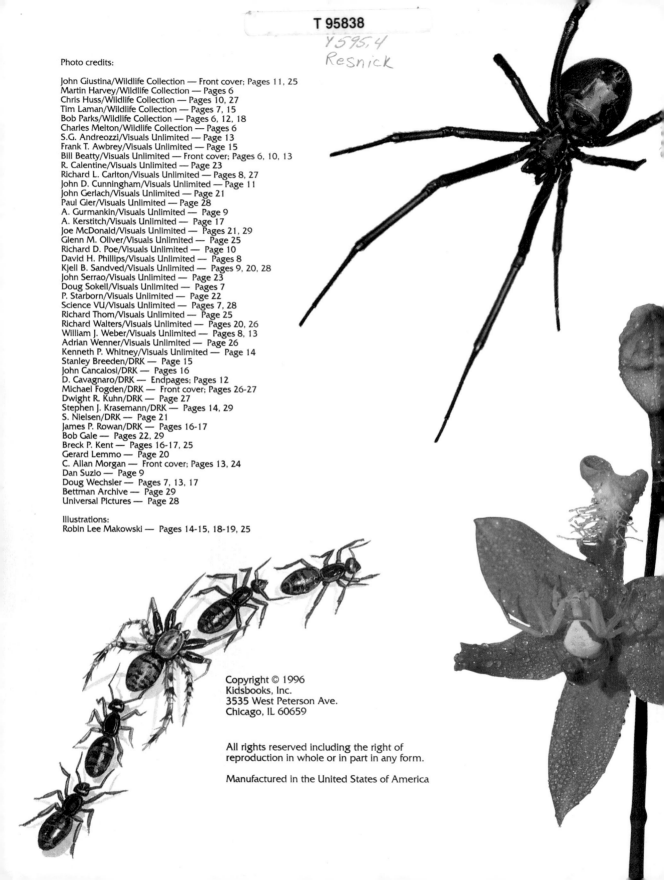

Photo credits:

John Giustina/Wildlife Collection — Front cover; Pages 11, 25
Martin Harvey/Wildlife Collection — Pages 6
Chris Huss/Wildlife Collection — Pages 10, 27
Tim Laman/Wildlife Collection — Pages 7, 15
Bob Parks/Wildlife Collection — Pages 6, 12, 18
Charles Melton/Wildlife Collection — Pages 6
S.G. Andreozzi/Visuals Unlimited — Page 13
Frank T. Awbrey/Visuals Unlimited — Page 15
Bill Beatty/Visuals Unlimited — Front cover; Pages 6, 10, 13
R. Calentine/Visuals Unlimited — Page 23
Richard L. Carlton/Visuals Unlimited — Pages 8, 27
John D. Cunningham/Visuals Unlimited — Page 11
John Gerlach/Visuals Unlimited — Page 21
Paul Gier/Visuals Unlimited — Page 28
A. Gurmankin/Visuals Unlimited — Page 9
A. Kerstitch/Visuals Unlimited — Page 17
Joe McDonald/Visuals Unlimited — Pages 21, 29
Glenn M. Oliver/Visuals Unlimited — Page 25
Richard D. Poe/Visuals Unlimited — Page 10
David H. Phillips/Visuals Unlimited — Pages 8
Kjell B. Sandved/Visuals Unlimited — Pages 9, 20, 28
John Serrao/Visuals Unlimited — Page 23
Doug Sokell/Visuals Unlimited — Pages 7
P. Starborn/Visuals Unlimited — Page 22
Science VU/Visuals Unlimited — Pages 7, 28
Richard Thom/Visuals Unlimited — Page 25
Richard Walters/Visuals Unlimited — Pages 20, 26
William J. Weber/Visuals Unlimited — Pages 8, 13
Adrian Wenner/Visuals Unlimited — Page 26
Kenneth P. Whitney/Visuals Unlimited — Page 14
Stanley Breeden/DRK — Page 15
John Cancalosi/DRK — Pages 16
D. Cavagnaro/DRK — Endpages; Pages 12
Michael Fogden/DRK — Front cover; Pages 26-27
Dwight R. Kuhn/DRK — Page 27
Stephen J. Krasemann/DRK — Pages 14, 29
S. Nielsen/DRK — Page 21
James P. Rowan/DRK — Pages 16-17
Bob Gale — Pages 22, 29
Breck P. Kent — Pages 16-17, 25
Gerard Lemmo — Page 20
C. Allan Morgan — Front cover; Pages 13, 24
Dan Suzio — Page 9
Doug Wechsler — Pages 7, 13, 17
Bettman Archive — Page 29
Universal Pictures — Page 28

Illustrations:
Robin Lee Makowski — Pages 14-15, 18-19, 25

EYES ON NATURE™

SPIDERS

Written by
Jane P. Resnick

kidsbooks®
Incorporated

SPIDERS!

Down in the basement or up in the attic, out in the desert or high in the mountains—spiders are everywhere. And they've been here on Earth for more than 380 million years. There are about 30,000 known species, and maybe as many as three times more yet to be discovered. They can be as big as 10 inches across or smaller than the head of a pin. And a few have a pretty poisonous bite, more potent than a rattlesnake's!

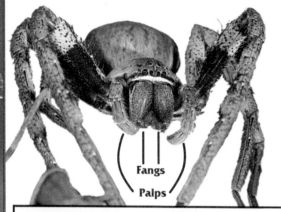

Fangs

Palps

DEADLY DENTURES

A spider's mouth is double trouble for prey. On each of its two jaws, a sharp, curved fang carries a poisonous bite. Then, on each side of the mouth are leglike things called *pedipalps*, or *palps*, which are used to hold prey.

HUNTERS AND TRAPPERS

All spiders are *carnivores*, or meat-eaters, that dine mostly on insects. Those known as wandering spiders are hunters that search for prey. The web builders, however, spin sticky traps of silk and lie in wait.

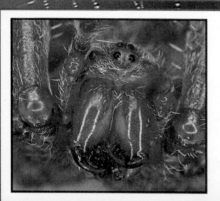

TRUE OR TARANTULA

Most common spiders are called "true spiders." Their jaws move from side to side (left). But the big, hairy spiders (right), most often called tarantulas in the United States, have large fangs and move their jaws up and down.

BACKBONES

What do you call an animal with legs and joints but no backbones? Scientists call them *arthropods* (ARE-thruh-pods). Like crabs, instead of having a skeleton on the inside, spiders have an *exoskeleton* on the outside, a tough suit of armor called a *carapace*, which protects the soft body parts.

SPIDERS VS. INSECTS

Spiders are not insects. Classified as *arachnids* (uh-RACK-nids), spiders have eight legs and two main parts to their body, and they can make silk. The arthropods known as *insects* are in the class *Insecta*. They have six legs, three main parts to their body, wings, and antennae.

◀ BREAK OUT

When a spider grows, its exoskeleton does not. So the spider molts. It replaces the small carapace with a bigger one. Depending on its size, a spider may molt from 3 to 12 times during its life. How does it do it? The spider hangs upside down by a silk thread until the exoskeleton splits, then simply pulls itself out, wearing a new carapace underneath.

▲ TWO-PARTS SPIDER

A spider's body is divided into two parts. The upper section is made up of the head, stomach, and poison glands. The lower section contains the heart, lungs, and other organs, as well as the silk glands.

FAMILY TIES

Every family has relatives. Spiders have scorpions and mites. These cousins have eight legs but different body types.

A scorpion raising its tail.

A mite, magnified.

7

SENSITIVE BODY

A leg with claw-like feet and sensitive hairs, magnified.

A long-legged wandering spider.

Spiders lack ears, so they do not hear as humans do. But they have legs that do a lot of "ear-work." Mostly on the legs, but also on the body, are hundreds of tiny slits that sense vibrations. With this leg sense, spiders know when an insect walks by or lands on a web.

▲ HAIRY SENSATIONS

Spiders feel objects they touch directly, and they also "feel" vibrations in the air, ground, and water. Sensory hairs are spread all over the spider's body. Each connects to nerves, which connect to the brain. Touch one hair, and the jumping spider (above) will know you're there.

SHED A LEG

If a leg is lost or damaged, spiders grow new ones. Sometimes spiders will shed a leg on purpose to escape a predator. The *regeneration*, or regrowth, of legs takes place as long as a spider is still molting.

▲ TASTE BY TOUCH

Putting their best foot forward, spiders taste  with their feet. Hollow hairs on the end of their legs and palps take in chemicals from food, and this produces taste. So when spiders hold or touch food, like this crab spider holding a bumblebee, they are probably tasting it.

EYE SIGHT

Most spiders have eight eyes! A few have six or four or less. All these eyes sit on the spider's face. Web builders have poor vision. But some hunting spiders can see well in several directions at once, like the amazing wolf spider (left), a creature that can spot objects a foot away!

HANGING ON ▼

A spider's legs are tools for balancing. Each one is flexible, with seven sections connected by joints. Wandering spiders have two claws and a tuft of hair on each foot to help them cling to slippery surfaces. Web builders, like this black widow, have three claws on each leg. The one in the middle grips fine silk strands.

▲ Fangs and palps

▶ This grasshopper will soon be soup.

LIQUID DIET

Liquids are all that spiders can eat, so they have to turn their prey to juice. Through their fangs, spiders inject victims with poison, then with digestive fluids. The prey's soft insides become like soup, and spiders can then suck up their meal.

SILKY WORLD

Silk emerges from an orb weaver's spinnerets.

A spider without silk is like a fish without water. Silk is the material of webs, traps, egg sacks, and burrow linings. It is produced by glands, as many as seven, deep inside a spider's body. It can be dry or sticky, fuzzy or smooth, thick or thin.

SILK SOURCE

Silk is still liquid as it leaves the spider's body. It emerges through *spinnerets*, which are flexible, fingerlike tubes, near the end of the body. As the spinnerets pull and bend the silk, the material hardens.

LIFELINE

Whenever they travel, spiders form a *dragline*, a double thread that trails behind them. With it, they can return home quickly and easily. If danger should approach, spiders use the dragline to escape, dropping out of sight and hanging on until the threat passes.

A black-and-yellow garden spider casting its dragline.

Amazonian spider

BUILDING BRIDGES

A silk bridge makes traveling between bushes and trees a lot easier. Standing in one place, spiders let out a thread for the wind to carry until it snags on another spot. Then the spider draws the strand tight and marches across, laying down more silk to strengthen the bridge.

WRAP IT UP

For humans, a silk-wrapped package is quite elegant. For spiders, it's dinner. Most spiders, after biting their prey, wrap the poisoned animal in silk threads. An insect bound in silk can be saved for a hungrier day.

Spiderlings preparing to balloon away.

THREADS OF STEEL

Silk may look fragile, but it's amazingly sturdy. Some types are three times stronger than a steel thread of the same diameter! Also, for added strength, spiders combine some threads to make thicker strands and may cover threads with a sticky substance. Silk is very flexible, too. Some can be stretched to nearly twice its length without breaking.

A spider web (in background) holds up easily under the strain of water droplets.

AIRBORNE

Silk is a baby spider's ticket to ride. Spiderlings spread out from one another by ballooning. They climb to a high place and point their spinnerets upward. Then they release a strand of silk, which is lifted by a stream of air, and off they go to live on their own, sometimes riding their silk line for 200 feet!

11

WONDER WEBS

Think of spider webs, and you may imagine a beautiful wheel with delicate spokes. This is the orb web, just one of the many kinds of webs that spiders build. The length of silk that goes into such a construction can be over 60 feet!

A banded garden spider on an orb web.

GOOD VIBES

Orb-web spiders have poor eyesight. But, tuned into vibrations on their web, they can tell the size and location of victims snared in their trap. When the prey is small, the spider dashes to attack. When large, the spider is more careful. If a wasp is caught, some spiders may cut the enemy loose rather than fight.

◄ With every leg on the net, this spider will know when prey has been snared.

▲ AMAZING ORB

Orb webs are the deadliest trap of all for flying insects. Orb spiders create this amazing structure of perfectly placed dry and sticky silk in less than an hour—every night! Then they remain head down in the web's center or go to a nearby silk retreat to wait for prey.

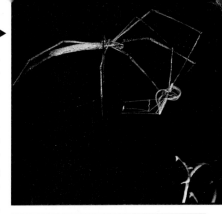

NO-NONSENSE NET ▶

Certain spiders can build elastic rectangular webs that fold up. The spider waits, holding the collapsed web like a net in its four *front* legs, hanging close to the ground by its four *back* legs. When insects pass by, the spider drops the net over its victims.

▲ A feast of trapped mayflies is waiting for the spider of this net.

◀ FUNNEL TUNNEL

Funnel weavers trap insects on the ground. They build tornado-shaped webs that are flat and lacy on the top with a funnel in the center. On the bottom, the spider waits. When it feels the vibrations of a passing insect, it races out to make the kill.

▼ HAMMOCK HUNTERS

Some spiders create hammock-shaped silk sheets on bushes or grass. Above, they run crisscrossing lines called scaffolding. Insects trapped in the scaffolding fall onto the hammock where the spider, waiting below, spears them with poison.

▲ WEB CITY

Not all spiders are loners. Social types live in colonies, numbering in the thousands. They create an enormous web that covers a tree, or they link webs to blanket a field. Members recognize each other by walking on the web with special vibrations.

13

NABBING PREY

All spiders have ways of capturing prey, but each species has its own method. Those spiders that don't wait around for something to fall into a web are more aggressive. And when they strike, they have the tools to fight. They don't have a sticky net that holds prey, but they do have large, powerful jaws with which they grip dinner.

◄ STALKERS

A jumping spider is the most successful active hunter of all the arachnids. It stalks prey the way a cat stalks mice. And when it pounces, it's on target nine times out of ten!

FISH FEEL ▼

Fishing spiders spend their days floating on the leaves of water plants. Dangling their legs over the side, they pick up the vibrations of small fish or insects struggling on the surface. They snatch this prey from the water. They may also "fish," wiggling a leg to look like a worm.

QUICK CATCH ▲

Purse-web spiders dig burrows and line them with silk. They extend the silk as a tube, like the finger of a glove, up to the surface of the ground. There, they cover it with dirt and bits of leaves. When prey passes over this trap, the spiders slash the tube and drag the victim inside.

SPIDER EAT SPIDER

Pirate spiders are spider eaters. They're too slow to hunt and can't build webs, but they must kill to eat. Web spiders are their victims. Masters of surprise, pirates sneak onto webs and attack with deadly venom.

◀ In the tropics, huntsman spiders are welcome in people's homes because they eat cockroaches. This one's eating a spider.

SPIT STICK ▼

Imagine a spider that pins its prey with spit! That's the spitting spider. It squirts two gummy streams as far away as two times its body length. While doing so, the spider shakes its jaws from side to side to create a cage of spit that holds the prey captive. Then the spider bites.

BOLD BOLAS ▲

The prize for capturing prey with the least amount of silk goes to the bolas spider. At twilight, the bolas waits for a moth to appear. Then it drops one short line with a sticky glob on the end. When the moth is struck, it's stuck!

TRAPDOOR

A trapdoor spider digs a burrow and lines it with silk, then builds a door on top. It stays inside, waiting for vibrations from a passing insect. Then it opens the door and attacks.

TARANTULA DANCE

BIRD EATER

The most gigantic spiders in the world, with 3-inch bodies and 10-inch leg spans, live in South America. The size of a dinner plate, these tarantulas go after some of the biggest prey. Known as bird-eating spiders, they most often attack nesting birds.

The Colombian purple-bloom birdeater.

Big, hairy spiders are called tarantulas. Their real name, however, is *mygalomorph* (MIG-uh-luh-morf). The true tarantula is the European wolf spider. Its tarantula name comes from the medieval Italian city of Taranto. The people there claimed that the bite of a spider made them dance wildly. The dance was called the tarantella, and the spider became the tarantula.

▼ What does the old carapace of a hairy mygalomorph look like when shed? A collapsed spider.

SENIOR SPIDER

Most spiders live less than a full year. But tarantulas don't even mature to adulthood until they are about 10 or 11 years old. Females may live more than 20 years. The males are not so lucky. They often get eaten by the females right after mating.

UP A TREE

Tarantulas are good at climbing, because, like other wandering spiders, they have pads of hair on their feet. While they're up in trees, they capture frogs, birds, and lizards. With their powerful jaws, they can even crush a small poisonous snake.

This Indian ornamental spider ▶ hangs on tightly to a waxy leaf.

▲ In the desert, fast-moving lizards are a favorite meal.

▲ This striped tarantula emerges from its burrow.

ON DEFENSE ▼

When trouble comes their way, tarantulas make themselves look even more fierce. They raise their front legs, throw themselves back, lift their heads, and expose their fearsome fangs. Now, that's scary!

▲ LOVED TO DEATH

Spiders, like all creatures, suffer when their habitats are destroyed. But the most endangered spider is one that is loved too much. Furry tarantulas, especially the Mexican red-kneed spider, have become so popular as pets, too many have been taken from the wild. Now, sales are being regulated, and some are bred in captivity.

STAYING ALIVE!

Spiders have predators, such as frogs, toads, lizards, birds, and wasps. Disappearing is often the best defense. Hiding is another. One way that spiders hide is by making themselves look like other things. This is called *mimicry*. But if a spider can't escape, a battle begins.

BACK OFF! ▼

Faced with a predator, some spiders take a stand. They raise their front legs and show their fangs, hoping this will be enough to frighten the attacker.

DROP OR DIE

Web-building spiders, high above the ground, use the dragline to drop off the web and out of sight.

FIGHT

Spiders don't get too friendly with one another. If two meet up, they're bound to fight. And it's a battle to the end.

◀ DIVE TO SURVIVE

The fishing spider has a hiding spot underwater. If threatened, it goes below the surface in a dive most spiders would not survive.

HAIRY SCARY

Some tarantulas have a hairy defense weapon. When threatened, the Chilean red-leg tarantula raises its lower body, vibrates its back legs, and scrapes off a mist of stinging, barbed hairs. In a cloud of these tiny hairs a predator's skin stings and its eyes water. Then it is sure to back off.

FIERCE FANGS ▲

Faced with an attacker, the American female lynx points her fangs toward the enemy and shoots a stream of stinging venom eight inches—over ten times her body length.

RUN! ▲

Fast-moving hunters like jumping spiders simply *run* from danger.

WASP DISGUISE ▲

With a lower body that looks like a wasp's head, and spinnerets that look like antennae, some spiders can imitate wasp enemies. What wasp predators see seems to be a wasp on the move. Actually, it's a spider walking backwards.

ANT ACT

Some spiders have the right color and a slim "waist" to help them look like ants. They move their front legs as "antennae" and run in antlike, zigzag fashion. Their disguise is so good, some live with real ants.

TRICKY SPIDERS

Green lynx spider

BEHIND THE BLADE

For the long-jawed orb weaver, posture is a life saver. Clinging to a blade of grass with one pair of legs, it lies head down and extends its other legs until they are straight and narrow. It simply becomes part of the grass until danger goes past.

STILL AS A STICK ▶

This spider from South America chooses to become part of a stick rather than face an attacker.

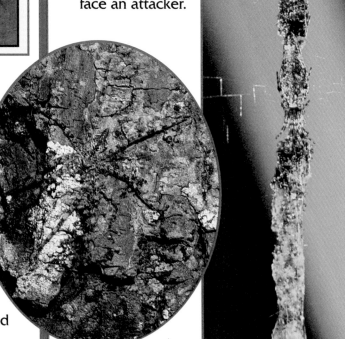

Camouflage, or blending into the background, fools both predators and prey. Predators pass by without noticing, and prey gets zapped with a deadly bite. Green lynx spiders know this trick. Their hunting grounds are always green, so they just sit still on green leaves and wait for dinner.

UNDERCOVER ▶

There are spiders that have markings like the lichen, mold, and mosses that grow on trees. Pressed up against a tree, flat as a pancake, these spiders blend in with the bark and cast no shadow.

▲ A goldenrod crab spider nabbing prey.

▲ A crab spider on a woodland sunflower.

▼ This crab spider gives a pink orchid a pretty center, where bees are likely to come looking for pollen.

The crab spider on these barberry blooms has snagged an unsuspecting fly.

FLOWER POWER

Crab spiders use the power of flowers to snare prey. Color is their weapon. Called flower spiders, they sit on flowers that match their body color. If their body is not just the right tone, they adjust it. Then they wait for a bee, butterfly, or even a fly to buzz by.

◄ The crab spider stays just below thistles until dinner arrives, and then, surprise!

21

SPIDERLINGS

There are billions upon billions of spiders on Earth, and more being born every minute. All female spiders lay eggs. Small spiders lay smaller and fewer eggs. Giant bird-eating spiders may lay up to 3,000 eggs, each the size of a pea.

BIG MAMAS ▶

Bigger is better for females in the spider world. The female's body has to hold eggs and produce silk to cover them. And she has to be big enough to protect her young. Some female orb-web spiders weigh as much as 1,000 times more than their mates.

In his courtship dance, the male jumping spider waves his front legs and trots sideways for the female.

◀ SIGN LANGUAGE

When female spiders add scent to their silk, males come running to mate. But a male has to be careful. A big lady spider could mistake a scrawny guy spider for a tasty meal. So, he sends signals. A male web spider may vibrate the silk strands of a female's web in a kind of code. Wandering spiders do a courtship dance.

MOTHER'S WORK ▶

Laying eggs and fertilizing them is the female spider's job. She deposits her eggs on a disc of silk and uses the fluid given to her by the male during mating to fertilize them. Then, like the nursery spider at right, she spins silk around the eggs to make a protective sac.

EGG-CESS BAGGAGE

Certain spiders protect their egg sac with their body. A crab spider (in circle) wraps her legs around her egg sac and stays there until she dies of starvation. The fishing spider (below) carries her sac beneath her body, clasped between her jaws and spinnerets. The sac is so big, the spider tiptoes on all eight legs.

▲ SAC HATCH

Spiderlings break out of their eggs and remain in their egg sac until they are fully developed. If they belong to a species without motherly care, they stay together for a short while. If food is scarce, they may eat a brother or sister before going on their way.

▼ BABY CARRIAGE

Newly hatched wolf spiderlings get a piggyback ride. Their mother cuts open the egg sac for them, and they scramble onto her back. If they fall off, they climb back up the draglines they have attached to her.

▲ NURSERY MOM

It's a dangerous world for spiderlings. But some spider mothers do take care of their young. The nursery-web spider builds a silk tent for her babies and guards them until they all scatter.

23

BAD BITES

Spiders bite. That's what fangs are for. And they do kill their prey with poison. A bite to humans, however, is almost always harmless, except when it's by the black widow, the brown recluse, or the Sydney funnel-web spider. But deaths from spiders are extremely rare.

The southern black widow has a red hourglass mark on the underside of its lower body.

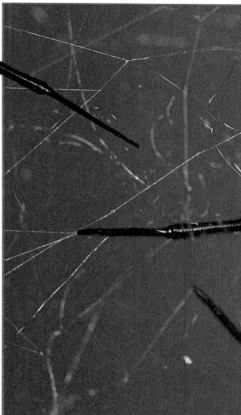

WIDOW'S WAYS

The female black widow spider has a bad reputation (males do not bite). Actually, she is a shy creature that likes dark places and runs if disturbed. She does live close to people, though. Found in clothes or shoes, she sometimes gets pressed against someone's bare skin. Frightened, she bites!

The much smaller male carefully approaches his mate.

DYING FOR LOVE

The black widow gets her name from killing her "husband" and making herself a widow. Indeed, she sometimes eats him. But male deaths are not a big loss for the species. They usually only mate once. And their bodies, having been eaten, provide nutrients for developing eggs.

VICIOUS VENOM

The black widow's venom is one of the deadliest. It's about 15 times more potent than rattlesnake venom, one of the more powerful snake toxins. Lucky for us, we are much larger than the black widow, and the amount of venom in her bite is small. So, several days of discomfort, rather than death, usually follow a bite from a black widow.

COBWEB WEAVER ▼

The black widow is not a very tidy spider. She hangs out around trash piles and dumps, and there she weaves a tangled, woolly mess, called a cobweb. She is one of many cobweb weavers who hang upside-down in the center of the web, waiting for prey to drop in. Then she sucks her victim dry.

◄ DANGER DOWN UNDER

Australia, which suffers from some of the most poisonous snakes in the world, has a spider to match, the Sydney funnel-web spider. Its bite at first causes unbearable pain. Then come convulsions and coma. Fortunately, a cure for the poison has been found.

Western widow

FRIGHTENING FAMILY

As if one were not enough, black widows have relatives. There are northern, western, brown, and red widows.

◄ WRETCHED RECLUSE

The brown recluse has a nasty poisonous bite that grows. It starts out as a small black spot, but the area of dead tissue increases, and six inches of skin can peel away. The victim is left with a wound that is hard to heal and a scar for a souvenir.

Northern widow

25

SPECIAL SELECTION

What you picture in your mind when you hear the word "spider" may not be what you actually see. Because there are so many species of spiders, you can be sure that they look very different from one another. Then, too, they don't all act the same. Here, you get a peek at an assortment of artful arthropods.

◀ Don't mistake them for insects! Microthena spiders have hard, spiny lower bodies, which are sometimes very colorful. This arrow-shaped microthena is found in gardens in the eastern United States.

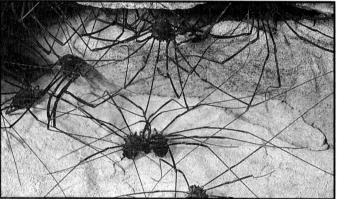

DISAPPEARING ACT ▲

Daddy-long-legs spiders look as frail as feathers, but they get around—especially in cellars and dark corners, where they hang upside-down in loose webs. If alarmed, the daddy-long-legs whirls around, shaking itself and its web so rapidly that they both seem to disappear.

◀ SAND SURFER ▶

The wheel spider of the South African desert travels like a wheel. Tucking in its eight legs to form a circle, the spider rolls away at amazing speeds. Because of the desert's smooth sand and steep dunes, the one-half inch spider can roll at 20 revolutions per second, the same as the wheel of a car traveling 137 miles per hour.

Wheel spider wheeling!

Wheel spider

WATER WORLD

Some spiders live in the water, trapping air bubbles they carry under the surface when they dive. European water spiders live under an air-filled silk tent. There are also about 600 species of sea spiders. They live near the shore or on the bottom of the ocean, where they feed on anemones and other sea creatures.

IN THE DARK ▶
What's a spider without eyes? A cave spider. This one lives in Malaysia.

The ▲ underwater home of a water spider.

LONG LEAP

Imagine jumping the length of a football field in a single bound. Jumping spiders make that kind of leap. Only a fifth of an inch long, they can jump 40 times their body length. They do it to eat. Jumping off strong back legs, they can even leap to catch flying insects in mid air!

◀ Captured in flight, this jumping spider will probably land on its prey.

LIVING WITH SPIDERS

Spiders can look pretty scary, with all those legs and eyes. Some people are really afraid of them. Really afraid. This fear is called arachnophobia (uh-RACK-nuh-foe-bee-uh). A movie by the same name certainly made the most of being afraid of spiders. But spiders aren't that big of a danger to people. They are actually a help.

◀ **STUDY A BUDDY**

Make your yard a spider home and be an *arachnologist*, a person who studies spiders. Let them build webs on bushes and trees. Don't disturb leaves and stones.

BITE FRIGHT

Getting bitten by a spider can be scary. But if you're healthy, most likely you'll be all right. However, you should go to a doctor. There are antidotes for black widow bites, and sometimes, when the bite is a bad one, pain killers are necessary.

The film that really played on spider terror was *The Incredible Shrinking Man*. Here's a scene where the little guy takes on a spider with a sewing needle.

▼ BUG BUSTER

Spiders eat so many insects, they could make good farmhands. In one experiment in California, wolf spiders consumed enough pests to increase a rice crop. If spiders can be introduced into fields to protect crops, they may be able to help decrease the use of pesticides.

A wolf spider snagging a cicada.

▼ MUFFET'S MEDICINE

Remember Miss Muffet and the spider who sat down beside her? She was a real girl, named Patience, who lived in the 1500s. Her father was a spider expert who made her eat mashed spiders when she was ill. Until the 1800s, many people believed spiders cured illness. They swallowed spiders like pills.

FIRST SPIDER

The name arachnid, for spiders, comes from a Greek legend. Arachne was a girl who outraged the goddess Athena with her beautiful weaving. Arachne became so upset over Athena's anger, she hanged herself. Athena, feeling sorry, turned Arachne into a spider so she could weave forever.

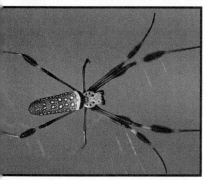

TOOLS OF SILK

People have found many uses for the silk spun by spiders. Silk from the golden silk spider has been used by people in the Caribbean to make fishing nets. Even this black-chinned hummingbird (right) has found that silk can be put to good use.

Golden silk spider

29